# Retirement Strategies

# For Millennials

*A Simple and Practical Plan for Retiring Early*

**REKHA CHIDIPOTHU**

To my beloved parents, Santha and Krishna

# INTRODUCTION

---

Are you a millennial just starting your career?

Do you wish to live the American dream?

Do you want financial freedom?

Are you one of the millions of Americans who desire to retire early?

If your answer is yes to any of the above questions, keep reading how to get there.

Do you believe that only the rich can retire early? If so, this book debunks that myth.

Early retirement is a possibility for everyone with a structured retirement savings plan regardless of income.

## What is a structured retirement savings plan?

A structured retirement savings plan is a disciplined and strategic way of growing your retirement savings to accumulate enough wealth for retiring early. You need to start early and regularly make contributions for retirement while ensuring your retirement contributions are getting invested in a diversified way.

As a first step, you can opt to sign up for a retirement plan, such as a 401(k), 403(b), 457(b), or Savings Incentive Match Plan for Employees (SIMPLE) IRA plan offered by your employer. Your retirement contributions automatically come out of your paycheck and go into the retirement plan. You need to figure out how much you will want to contribute to the retirement plan each year. Would you like to know a good strategy you can follow? Start early with a small retirement savings contribution and increase it by a set percentage each year to achieve your retirement goal.

Suppose you are making an annual income of 40,000

dollars, and you are 25 years old. You can save 10% or 4,000 dollars of your annual income each year and increase the savings by 1% of the initial investment or 400 dollars each year. With diversified investing and assuming a 7% annual return, you can have a nest egg of about one million dollars by 58 years old.

You may be curious about what it means to invest in a diversified way. Diversified investing minimizes your risk of losing money while maximizing your investment gains. Diversification means not putting all of your eggs in one basket. For example, if you invest all of your retirement savings in individual stocks, that will pose a significant risk. Instead, investing in a diversified mix of stocks and bonds or choosing Target Date Retirement funds tailored for retirement can minimize the risk.

Diversified investment of your retirement savings over a long time with the "compounding effect" does the magic for you to retire early. Would you like to know what the compounding effect is? Your investment gains from the preceding period are reinvested or remain invested to generate additional investment gains over time. In other words, you are generating investment gains from previous investment gains. For example, suppose you invest 10,000 dollars at a 7% annual return. Your investment gains will be 700 dollars with a savings balance of 10,700 dollars by the end of the first year. Your investment gains will be reinvested at a 7% return along with the principal. So, you will have investment gains of 749 dollars and a savings balance of 11,449 dollars by the end of the second year. At this rate of return, with a compounding effect, your money will become almost double in 10 years.

Did you know that your employer-sponsored retirement plan has significant tax benefits? A lot of employers offer 401(k), 403(b), or 457(b) plans for their employees. If you sign up for one of these plans, you can choose to contribute pre-tax dollars or after-tax dollars to your retirement plan. The option to contribute after-tax dollars to these plans is known as a Roth option. In the case of a pre-tax contribution, you contribute the amount on which you have not paid taxes. For an after-tax contribution, you contribute the amount on which you have paid taxes.

Suppose you contribute pre-tax dollars to your retirement plan; your contributions will grow tax-deferred. You will be paying taxes on your contributions and investment gains when you withdraw funds from your retirement plan. Alternatively, suppose you contribute after-tax dollars to your retirement plan. In that scenario, you need not pay any taxes on your contributions or your investment gains when you withdraw funds from your retirement plan.

So, how do you choose whether to contribute pre-tax dollars or after-tax dollars to your 401(k), 403(b), or 457(b) plan? The contribution of pre-tax dollars can be a good strategy if you think you will be in a lower tax bracket during your retirement years. A lower tax bracket means paying taxes at a lower tax rate because you will have lesser taxable income. So, in this case, you will not pay taxes now but pay lower taxes during your retirement.

On the other hand, contributing after-tax dollars to your

retirement plan can be beneficial if you anticipate being in a higher tax bracket during your retirement years. A higher tax bracket implies paying taxes at a higher tax rate as you will have more taxable income. You may lose some tax credits or deductions and end up with higher taxable income during your retirement. So, in this scenario, you would rather pay taxes now and have your money be tax-free during your retirement years.

Alternatively, some employers offer SIMPLE IRA or Simplified Employee Pension (SEP) plans for their employees. These plans allow pre-tax contributions only. Suppose you have signed up for a SIMPLE IRA plan; you or your employer will be able to contribute pre-tax dollars to your retirement plan. Alternatively, if your employer offers a SEP plan, only your employer can make pre-tax contributions for your retirement. For SIMPLE IRA and SEP plans, your retirement contributions and investment gains grow tax-deferred. However, you will be required to pay taxes on your contributions and investment gains when you withdraw funds from your retirement plan during the retirement years.

Have you found out if your employer will match your retirement contributions? The vast majority of employers offer to match your contributions to the retirement savings plan up to a set percentage of your salary. If your employer does offer to match your retirement contributions, then you are in luck. For example, suppose your annual income is 40,000 dollars; your employer matches 100% of your retirement contributions up to 5% of your salary. In that case, your employer will contribute 5% or 2,000 dollars each year to your retirement plan, provided your contribution is at least 2,000 dollars.

On the other hand, suppose you opt to contribute only 3% or 1,200 dollars when the employer match is up to 5%. In that scenario, your employer will contribute only 3% or 1,200 dollars matching your contribution. So, it is in your best interest to take full advantage of the employer match and contribute at least 5% or 2,000 dollars in this case to boost your retirement savings.

Did you know that how much you can contribute to the

employer-sponsored retirement plan has a maximum limit? You can contribute only up to a specific maximum limit to your employer-sponsored retirement plan. The maximum limit on your contributions to the retirement plan can change each year as the law keeps changing. For example, you can contribute a maximum of 19,500 dollars to the employer-sponsored 401(k), 403(b), or 457(b) plan for 2021. However, there is a catch-up contribution limit of additional 6,500 dollars for individuals aged 50 and older. For the SIMPLE IRA plan, you can contribute a maximum of 13,500 dollars for 2021. A catch-up contribution of additional 3,000 dollars for individuals aged 50 and older is allowed for the SIMPLE IRA plan. In the case of the SEP plan, you do not have the option to make contributions. Your employer can contribute up to a maximum of 25% of your compensation or 58,000 dollars, whichever is less for 2021.

One good point is that the maximum limit noted above for a 401(k) or 403(b) does not include what the employer matches for your contributions. Suppose you contribute the maximum allowed 19,500 dollars to your 401(k) plan yearly;

what your employer matches is 3,000 dollars. A total of 22,500 dollars go into your retirement plan each year, and that helps to grow your retirement nest egg. The maximum limit on the total of your contributions and your employer contributions to your 401(k) or 403(b) plan is 58,000 dollars or your compensation, whichever is less for 2021.

Have you heard about individual retirement arrangements such as a Traditional IRA or Roth IRA? Similar to the employer-sponsored plan, the Traditional IRA and Roth IRA accounts have tax benefits and effectively supplement your savings in the employer-sponsored retirement plan.

With the Traditional IRA, you contribute pre-tax dollars, and your retirement savings grow tax-deferred. Additionally, you may be eligible to receive tax deduction savings upfront for your Traditional IRA contribution when you file your income taxes. You pay taxes on the Traditional IRA contributions and investment gains when you withdraw your funds. The Traditional IRA can be a good option if you anticipate being in a lower tax bracket during your retirement years or are eligible for tax deduction savings.

With the Roth IRA option, you will make contributions with after-tax dollars. The contributions and investment gains from the Roth IRA account will be tax-free when you withdraw funds, and it can be a good option if you anticipate being in a higher tax bracket during retirement.

As in the case of employer-sponsored plans, how much you can contribute to the Traditional IRA and Roth IRA has a maximum limit. For example, for 2021, the Traditional IRA or Roth IRA's maximum limit is 6,000 dollars for individuals under age 50 and 7,000 dollars for individuals aged 50 and older. However, you can only contribute up to your taxable compensation if your taxable compensation is less than the maximum limit.

If possible, you should contribute the maximum allowed to your employer-sponsored retirement savings plan and IRA account because there are significant tax benefits.

Keep in mind that if you withdraw your savings from your employer-sponsored retirement plan (except for the 457 plan) or IRA accounts before you turn 59½, you may need to pay a penalty of 10% in most cases. Therefore, avoid withdrawing your retirement savings from your employer-sponsored retirement plan or IRA accounts prematurely to let your retirement savings compound for the long term.

Are you self-employed and wondering about what would be your options for saving for retirement? You have many of the same retirement plan options as the employees to save for retirement. You can contribute to a 401(k), SIMPLE IRA, or SEP plan. If you choose the 401(k) option, you will be able to contribute additional savings to your retirement plan as an employer and employee.

For a 401(k) plan, if you are self-employed, you can contribute up to a maximum  allowed for the retirement plan as with the case of an employee. In addition, being an employer, you can contribute as much as 25% of your net earnings for 2021. For example, suppose you are self-employed under age 50, and your net earnings are 40,000 dollars. In that case, you can contribute 25% of 40,000 dollars which is 10,000 dollars, plus the maximum allowed employee contribution for the 401(k) plan, which is 19,500 dollars totaling 29,500 dollars. For the self-employed, the maximum limit for your retirement contributions in the 401(k) plan is 58,000 dollars for 2021.

For the SEP plan, if you are self-employed, you can contribute up to 25% of your net earnings not exceeding 58,000 dollars for 2021. However, if you have employees, you need to contribute to their retirement plans at the same rate you have contributed to your retirement plan. For example, suppose you are self-employed, and you contribute 10% of your earnings to your retirement plan. You will need to make a contribution of 10% of your employee's salary to your employee's retirement plan.

For the SIMPLE IRA plan, if you are self-employed, you can contribute to the plan up to the maximum allowed limit of 13,500 dollars plus an additional 3,000 dollars if you are

50 years of age or older. Additionally, you can contribute a fixed 2% or match up to 3% of your salary in your retirement plan for 2021. If you have employees, they can contribute up to the same maximum allowed limit. Additionally, as an employer, you need to contribute a fixed 2% or match up to 3% of the employee's salary. You can choose either the fixed or matching contribution, but the contribution rate must be the same for you and your employees.

How do you choose which retirement plan is the best for you if you are self-employed? SIMPLE IRA and SEP plans are easier to set up and maintain with fewer administrative costs than the 401(k) plan. A SEP plan is a good option if your business is cyclical with good times and downtimes. You can make more significant contributions during good times and lesser contributions during bad times. A SIMPLE IRA plan is a good choice if you have employees. You may want your employees to share the responsibility for their retirement. A Solo 401(k) plan may be an excellent option if you do not have employees. You can contribute to your retirement plan in the employer and employee capacity. With a Solo 401(k) plan, you can contribute pre-tax or after-tax dollars just like the regular 401(k). If you have more than 100 employees, you can consider the 401(k) option.

Finally, increasing the contributions to the retirement savings plan can be challenging with a tight budget. In that case, you may be able to invest any of your yearly salary increases or bonuses to avoid a dip in your take-home pay.

# CHAPTER ONE

# Start Early to Save for Retirement

Would you like to know the most simple yet powerful strategy for retiring early? Start as early as possible to save for retirement because the power of compounding plays a huge role in growing your retirement savings. The longer the time horizon, the more opportunity your money gets to grow.

As an example, if you save 5,000 dollars each year for 30 years with a 7% annual return, you will accumulate 472,304 dollars. On the other hand, if you save double that, 10,000 dollars each year for 15 years with the same 7% annual return, you will end up with only 251,290 dollars.

You may be young, and you might have started your first job. You may think you have ample time to save for retirement. However, you should save for retirement right from day one when you start working. Starting with small yearly retirement contributions sooner is better than bigger yearly contributions closer to retirement.

For example, John starts to save for retirement when he is 25 years old and contributes 6,000 dollars each year. With a

7% annual return, his retirement savings will be 829,421 dollars by the time he turns 59 years old.

Tom starts to save for retirement at the age of 45 and contributes three times more each year which is 18,000 dollars. With a 7% annual return, his retirement savings will be only 452,322 dollars by the time he turns 59 years old.

Are you wondering how John could save almost double what Tom saved for his retirement with lesser contributions?

The following chart shows how the compounding effect over a long period dramatically increased John's savings even though his yearly retirement contribution of 6,000 dollars is one-third of Tom's annual contribution of 18,000 dollars.

## John's Retirement Plan

| Age | Contribution | Savings Balance |
|-----|--------------|-----------------|
| 25 | $6,000 | $6,000 |
| 26 | $6,000 | $12,420 |
| 27 | $6,000 | $19,289 |
| 28 | $6,000 | $26,640 |
| 29 | $6,000 | $34,504 |
| 30 | $6,000 | $42,920 |
| 31 | $6,000 | $51,924 |
| 32 | $6,000 | $61,559 |
| 33 | $6,000 | $71,868 |
| 34 | $6,000 | $82,899 |
| 35 | $6,000 | $94,702 |
| 36 | $6,000 | $107,331 |
| 37 | $6,000 | $120,844 |
| 38 | $6,000 | $135,303 |
| 39 | $6,000 | $150,774 |
| 40 | $6,000 | $167,328 |
| 41 | $6,000 | $185,041 |
| 42 | $6,000 | $203,994 |
| 43 | $6,000 | $224,274 |
| 44 | $6,000 | $245,973 |
| 45 | $6,000 | $269,191 |
| 46 | $6,000 | $294,034 |
| 47 | $6,000 | $320,617 |
| 48 | $6,000 | $349,060 |
| 49 | $6,000 | $379,494 |
| 50 | $6,000 | $412,059 |
| 51 | $6,000 | $446,903 |
| 52 | $6,000 | $484,186 |
| 53 | $6,000 | $524,079 |
| 54 | $6,000 | $566,765 |
| 55 | $6,000 | $612,438 |
| 56 | $6,000 | $661,309 |
| 57 | $6,000 | $713,601 |
| 58 | $6,000 | $769,553 |
| 59 | $6,000 | $829,421 |

## Tom's Retirement Plan

| Age | Contribution | Savings Balance |
|:---:|:---:|:---:|
| 45 | $18,000 | $18,000 |
| 46 | $18,000 | $37,260 |
| 47 | $18,000 | $57,868 |
| 48 | $18,000 | $79,919 |
| 49 | $18,000 | $103,513 |
| 50 | $18,000 | $128,759 |
| 51 | $18,000 | $155,772 |
| 52 | $18,000 | $184,676 |
| 53 | $18,000 | $215,604 |
| 54 | $18,000 | $248,696 |
| 55 | $18,000 | $284,105 |
| 56 | $18,000 | $321,992 |
| 57 | $18,000 | $362,532 |
| 58 | $18,000 | $405,909 |
| 59 | $18,000 | $452,322 |

You may find it interesting to see that John contributed a total of 210,000 dollars, less than the total contributions Tom made the 270,000 dollars. However, John has accumulated 829,421 dollars, whereas Tom has accumulated 452,322 dollars. In a nutshell, even though John has contributed less than Tom, John has amassed almost double that of Tom by saving earlier for retirement.

## That is the power of compounding!

Maybe you are starting your career and feel you cannot afford a big chunk of money going into your retirement plan. In that case, a good strategy would be to start with a small yearly contribution to your retirement plan. You may be able to increase it by a set percentage each year as your annual income grows.

Many employer-sponsored retirement plans let you sign up for an automatic increase in your retirement contributions each year. You might want to consider signing up if you have that option, so you will reach your retirement goal faster.

For example, Peter is 25 years old with an annual income of 40,000 dollars. He saves 10% or 4,000 dollars of his income each year and increases the savings by 1% or 400 dollars each year. With a 7% yearly return, Peter will have a retirement nest egg of 1 million dollars by the age of 58 years old. See the following chart.

## Peter's Retirement Plan

| Age | Contribution | Savings Balance |
|:---:|:---:|:---:|
| 25 | $4,000 | $4,000 |
| 26 | $4,400 | $8,680 |
| 27 | $4,800 | $14,088 |
| 28 | $5,200 | $20,274 |
| 29 | $5,600 | $27,293 |
| 30 | $6,000 | $35,203 |
| 31 | $6,400 | $44,068 |
| 32 | $6,800 | $53,952 |
| 33 | $7,200 | $64,929 |
| 34 | $7,600 | $77,074 |
| 35 | $8,000 | $90,469 |
| 36 | $8,400 | $105,202 |
| 37 | $8,800 | $121,366 |
| 38 | $9,200 | $139,062 |
| 39 | $9,600 | $158,396 |
| 40 | $10,000 | $179,484 |
| 41 | $10,400 | $202,448 |
| 42 | $10,800 | $227,419 |
| 43 | $11,200 | $254,539 |
| 44 | $11,600 | $283,956 |
| 45 | $12,000 | $315,833 |
| 46 | $12,400 | $350,341 |
| 47 | $12,800 | $387,665 |
| 48 | $13,200 | $428,002 |
| 49 | $13,600 | $471,562 |
| 50 | $14,000 | $518,571 |
| 51 | $14,400 | $569,271 |
| 52 | $14,800 | $623,920 |
| 53 | $15,200 | $682,795 |
| 54 | $15,600 | $746,190 |
| 55 | $16,000 | $814,424 |
| 56 | $16,400 | $887,833 |
| 57 | $16,800 | $966,782 |
| 58 | $17,200 | $1,051,657 |

So, save early for retirement and let your retirement savings compound over a long time. You can start with a small contribution but increase it by a set percentage each year. This approach will help you to retire early.

# CHAPTER TWO

# Invest in a Well-Diversified
# Portfolio of Stocks and Bonds

By now, you know the power of compounding, and maybe you are interested in investing your retirement savings for a long term to retire early. Are you curious about how to invest your retirement savings so you can grow your money without a significant risk of losing money?

The answer is diversified investing, which means not putting all your eggs in one basket. Diversified investing is a strategy that minimizes the risk of losing money by investing in a varied pool of assets, such as cash, domestic and foreign stocks, and bonds.

Suppose you invest all your retirement savings and buy the stocks of a single company XYZ. If that company goes bankrupt in the future, you will lose a lot of your money. On the other hand, let us say you invest your money in a mutual fund comprising stocks and bonds of many top-performing companies, domestic and foreign, in various sectors. Your investment risk is less than that of investing all your money in the stock of an individual company. Even if one of the companies in the fund does not do well, your risk is mitigated by some other companies in the fund doing well.

You may know that an investment portfolio is a collection of stocks and bonds that you may have invested your money in. You can pick an investment strategy that best suits your risk tolerance level. Typically, stocks have higher risk and higher returns than bonds. So, an aggressive investment strategy entails having an investment portfolio with a higher percentage of stocks and a lower percentage of bonds. A more conservative investment strategy dictates an investment portfolio with fewer stocks and more bonds.

Did you know most employer-sponsored retirement plans offer Target Date Retirement funds? You can consider the Target Date Retirement fund as a good option for investing your retirement savings. Target Date Retirement funds are a series of funds, each one tailored to a specific retirement year. You would choose a Target Date Retirement fund based on the year you would like to retire. For example, you can pick the 2050 Target Date Retirement fund if you plan to retire in 2050. Typically, the Target Date Retirement fund is comprised of a diversified mix of domestic and foreign stocks and bonds. As we noted earlier, typically, investing in stocks provides higher risk and return potential than investing in bonds. The Target Date Retirement funds are rebalanced each year automatically so that the ratio of stocks and bonds is adjusted to your age. When retirement is in the distant future, much of your money gets invested in stocks, and less in bonds as your risk tolerance would be higher. As you approach your retirement, much of your money will be invested more in bonds and less in stocks because your risk tolerance will be lower.

An essential factor to consider when choosing a mutual fund is the cost of the fund. Based on the sales fees charged, mutual funds can be front-end load funds, back-end load funds, or no-load funds. For the front-end load funds, you would pay a sales charge up front when you buy the fund, whereas, for the back-end load funds, you would pay a sales charge when you sell the shares of your fund. No sales charge is associated with the no-load funds. However, other fees may be associated even with the no-load funds, such as administration, management, and advertising expenses. The expense ratio of the fund indicates these fees. For example, if you invested 10,000 dollars for 20 years in a no-load fund that has an expense ratio of 1% and yields a 7% annual return, the fees will cost you a total of 7,047 dollars. Therefore, choose low-cost funds with low expense ratios for investing your money because the fees will, in effect, reduce your investment gains.

Typically, you cannot withdraw the retirement savings in tax-advantaged employer-sponsored plan and IRA accounts before you reach the age of 59½ without incurring a penalty. Are you wondering what plan to follow if you would like to retire even sooner, maybe at age 50? Would you like to know a couple of strategies you could use to retire sooner than 59½ years old? Suppose you choose to retire and separate from service with your employer anytime during or after you turn 55 years old. In that case, you need not pay the penalty to withdraw from your 401(k) plan with that employer. Alternatively, you can supplement your savings in your retirement accounts by investing in taxable accounts, preferably after maxing out your retirement accounts.

Taxable accounts are your cash accounts and brokerage accounts. You can invest your money in a non-retirement account, such as a taxable brokerage account. These accounts have no maximum limit on how much you can invest compared to your retirement accounts. However, the taxable accounts do not have the tax benefits of a retirement account. You would be required to invest your after-tax dollars and pay the tax on your investment gains when you sell your shares. You will want to note the difference between realized and unrealized investment gains. Your investment gains are unrealized prior to selling your shares and realized upon selling your shares. The tax on the realized investment gains is known as the capital gains tax. After your purchase, if you hold your investments for more than a year, the capital gains tax rate is lower and is referred to as the long-term capital gains tax rate. Based on your income and income tax filing status, the long-term capital gains tax rate is 0%, 15%, or 20% for 2021 year. If you sell your investments within one year or sooner, the capital gains tax rate applied is the short-term capital gains tax rate. It is equivalent to the ordinary income tax rate as per the current law. Unlike the retirement accounts, you will be able to sell your investments in the taxable accounts any time you choose without incurring a penalty. Hence, it is beneficial to supplement your retirement savings in your retirement accounts with additional savings in taxable accounts if you want to retire before turning 59½ years old.

Apart from taxable accounts, the other types of accounts you may want to know about are tax-deferred accounts and tax-free accounts. Tax-deferred accounts are retirement plans, such as Traditional 401(k) plan and Traditional IRA. As introduced earlier, you can contribute pre-tax dollars to the Traditional 401(k) plan and Traditional IRA, and your contributions will grow tax-deferred. You will pay taxes on your contributions and investment gains when you withdraw funds from the tax-deferred accounts during your retirement. The tax-free accounts are retirement plans, such as Roth 401(k) plan and Roth IRA. You can contribute after-tax dollars to Roth 401(k) plan and Roth IRA as noted earlier.

You will not pay taxes on your contributions and investment gains when you withdraw funds from the tax-free accounts during your retirement.

Are you interested in hiring a financial advisor for your retirement needs? A financial advisor will provide you with the investment advice to pick the suitable funds and asset mix for your retirement portfolio based on your risk tolerance level. However, there is a cost associated with hiring a financial advisor. Financial advisor charges can be fee-based or commission-based. Fee-based financial advisors charge a flat fee as a percentage of your total investment assets. Suppose you have investment assets of 100,000 dollars, and the financial advisor charges a 1% fee annually; you will be paying 1,000 dollars each year for the financial advisor for managing your investment portfolio. Commission-based financial advisors do not charge fees, but they get paid by brokerage firms for selling the investment products to you. So, be wary that the commission-based financial advisors may have an incentive behind their investment advice because they get commissions for selling specific investment products.

Assuming you have invested in a diversified way, you must stay invested through the up and down cycles of the stock market. Even if the market underperforms in one year, historically, the market will recover in the following years. Therefore, it is not prudent to sell your retirement investments when the market underperforms in a particular year. Remember, you need to keep your retirement savings invested over the long term to grow your retirement nest egg.

# CHAPTER THREE

# Take Advantage of the Employer's Matching of Retirement Contributions

Would you like to know about a valuable employee benefit a lot of employers offer that will help you to retire early? It is the employer matching your retirement contributions. Most employers offer to match your contributions to your retirement savings plan up to a set percentage of your salary.

Why is this a valuable employee benefit?

Suppose you want to retire early; your goal is to contribute 15% of your annual income to your employer-sponsored retirement savings plan. Let us say your employer match is up to 5% of your salary. You can contribute 10% of your annual income, and your employer match is 5% making up for the rest. Therefore, your employer is helping you meet your retirement goal by making one-third of your total annual contributions in this case.

Thus, the employer match helps to ramp up your retirement savings; you can grow your retirement nest egg faster and retire sooner.

For example, Ruth is making an annual income of 40,000 dollars, and she wants to save 20% or 8,000 dollars of her income each year to retire early. Assume Ruth has a tight budget which allows savings of a maximum of 15% or 6,000 dollars each year. Luckily, her employer matches 100% of her contributions up to 5% of her salary. She will meet her retirement goal of saving 8,000 dollars each year with an employer match equivalent to 2,000 dollars. With a 7% annual return, Ruth will have a nest egg of about a million dollars by 58 years old. This is illustrated in the chart to the right.

In this case, Ruth's employer is contributing one-fourth of the yearly retirement contributions to her retirement savings plan, Ruth will be able to meet her retirement goal faster with her employer matching her contributions to her retirement savings plan.

# Ruth's Retirement Plan

| Age | Contribution | Employer Match | Savings Balance |
|-----|-------------|----------------|-----------------|
| 25 | $6,000 | $2,000 | $8,000 |
| 26 | $6,000 | $2,000 | $16,560 |
| 27 | $6,000 | $2,000 | $25,719 |
| 28 | $6,000 | $2,000 | $35,520 |
| 29 | $6,000 | $2,000 | $46,006 |
| 30 | $6,000 | $2,000 | $57,226 |
| 31 | $6,000 | $2,000 | $69,232 |
| 32 | $6,000 | $2,000 | $82,078 |
| 33 | $6,000 | $2,000 | $95,824 |
| 34 | $6,000 | $2,000 | $110,532 |
| 35 | $6,000 | $2,000 | $126,269 |
| 36 | $6,000 | $2,000 | $143,108 |
| 37 | $6,000 | $2,000 | $161,125 |
| 38 | $6,000 | $2,000 | $180,404 |
| 39 | $6,000 | $2,000 | $201,032 |
| 40 | $6,000 | $2,000 | $223,104 |
| 41 | $6,000 | $2,000 | $246,722 |
| 42 | $6,000 | $2,000 | $271,992 |
| 43 | $6,000 | $2,000 | $299,032 |
| 44 | $6,000 | $2,000 | $327,964 |
| 45 | $6,000 | $2,000 | $358,921 |
| 46 | $6,000 | $2,000 | $392,046 |
| 47 | $6,000 | $2,000 | $427,489 |
| 48 | $6,000 | $2,000 | $465,413 |
| 49 | $6,000 | $2,000 | $505,992 |
| 50 | $6,000 | $2,000 | $549,412 |
| 51 | $6,000 | $2,000 | $595,871 |
| 52 | $6,000 | $2,000 | $645,582 |
| 53 | $6,000 | $2,000 | $698,772 |
| 54 | $6,000 | $2,000 | $755,686 |
| 55 | $6,000 | $2,000 | $816,584 |
| 56 | $6,000 | $2,000 | $881,745 |
| 57 | $6,000 | $2,000 | $951,467 |
| 58 | $6,000 | $2,000 | $1,026,070 |

The employer matching contributions may only vest over a period of time. This period, if any, varies by employer. Therefore, you should stay with your employer until the employer's matching contributions are vested.

Although many employers offer to match retirement contributions, not all employers match up to 100% of your retirement contributions. Some employers may match only up to 50%, and some others may match up to even higher than 100%. The most common employer match is typically 50% of retirement contributions up to 6% of an employee's salary.

For example, Jeff's annual income is 40,000 dollars. He contributes 15% or 6,000 dollars each year to his retirement savings plan with a 50% employer match up to 6% of his salary. In other words, Jeff's employer is contributing 1,200 dollars to his retirement savings plan each year through the employer match. With a 7% annual return, Jeff will have a nest egg close to a million dollars by 59 years old. See the chart on the right.

## Jeff's Retirement Plan

| Age | Contribution | Employer Match | Savings Balance |
|-----|--------------|----------------|-----------------|
| 25 | $6,000 | $1,200 | $7,200 |
| 26 | $6,000 | $1,200 | $14,904 |
| 27 | $6,000 | $1,200 | $23,147 |
| 28 | $6,000 | $1,200 | $31,968 |
| 29 | $6,000 | $1,200 | $41,405 |
| 30 | $6,000 | $1,200 | $51,504 |
| 31 | $6,000 | $1,200 | $62,309 |
| 32 | $6,000 | $1,200 | $73,871 |
| 33 | $6,000 | $1,200 | $86,242 |
| 34 | $6,000 | $1,200 | $99,478 |
| 35 | $6,000 | $1,200 | $113,642 |
| 36 | $6,000 | $1,200 | $128,797 |
| 37 | $6,000 | $1,200 | $145,013 |
| 38 | $6,000 | $1,200 | $162,364 |
| 39 | $6,000 | $1,200 | $180,929 |
| 40 | $6,000 | $1,200 | $200,794 |
| 41 | $6,000 | $1,200 | $222,050 |
| 42 | $6,000 | $1,200 | $244,793 |
| 43 | $6,000 | $1,200 | $269,129 |
| 44 | $6,000 | $1,200 | $295,168 |
| 45 | $6,000 | $1,200 | $323,029 |
| 46 | $6,000 | $1,200 | $352,841 |
| 47 | $6,000 | $1,200 | $384,740 |
| 48 | $6,000 | $1,200 | $418,872 |
| 49 | $6,000 | $1,200 | $455,393 |
| 50 | $6,000 | $1,200 | $494,471 |
| 51 | $6,000 | $1,200 | $536,284 |
| 52 | $6,000 | $1,200 | $581,023 |
| 53 | $6,000 | $1,200 | $628,895 |
| 54 | $6,000 | $1,200 | $680,118 |
| 55 | $6,000 | $1,200 | $734,926 |
| 56 | $6,000 | $1,200 | $793,571 |
| 57 | $6,000 | $1,200 | $856,321 |
| 58 | $6,000 | $1,200 | $923,463 |
| 59 | $6,000 | $1,200 | $995,306 |

In this scenario, Jeff's employer is contributing one-sixth of the yearly contributions to his retirement savings plan through the employer match. So, the employer match helps Jeff to grow his retirement savings faster to retire early.

In the case of the 401(k) and 403(b) plans, the total of your contributions and employer matching contributions cannot exceed your salary or 58,000 dollars, whichever is less for 2021. For a SIMPLE IRA plan, the employer contribution can be a fixed 2% or a matching contribution of up to 3% of your annual salary.

Keep in mind that you need to contribute to your retirement savings plan at least as much as your employer match to take full advantage of your employer match. For example, suppose you are making an annual income of 40,000 dollars. Your employer match is 100% of your retirement contributions up to 4% of your salary. In this case, your employer will contribute 4% or 1,600 dollars each year to your retirement plan, provided your contribution is at least 1,600 dollars.

On the other hand, suppose you choose to contribute only 3% or 1,200 dollars, when your employer match is up to 4%. Your employer will contribute only 3% or 1,200 dollars that matches your contribution. So, you should take full advantage of your employer match and contribute at least 4% or 1,600 dollars in this case to boost your retirement savings.

Remember, you need to contribute to your employer-sponsored retirement plan at the least to the full extent of your employer match.

—

**CHAPTER FOUR**

---

# Supplement the Savings in an Employer-Sponsored Plan with IRA Contributions

---

Are you interested in finding out yet another simple strategy for growing your retirement savings to retire early? Did you know you can contribute each year to Individual Retirement Account (IRA) to supplement the retirement savings in your employer-sponsored plan? An IRA is another powerful vehicle to grow your retirement savings. An IRA can be Traditional or Roth, and both types have significant tax benefits.

You can open Traditional IRA or Roth IRA at a bank, other financial institutions, with a mutual fund, life insurance company, or through your stockbroker.

You could make contributions to a Traditional IRA or Roth IRA if you received taxable compensation during the year. Generally, compensation is what you earn from working and does not include income, such as rental income, interest income, dividend income, pension, or annuity income.

You can find what is considered compensation for the purposes of an IRA in the following table.

## Compensation for purposes of an IRA

| Includes | Doesn't include |
|---|---|
| Wages, salaries, etc. | Earnings and profits from property |
| Commissions | Interest and dividend income |
| Self-employment income | Pension or annuity income |
| Taxable alimony and separate maintenance | Deferred compensation |
| Non-taxable combat pay | Income from certain partnerships |
| Taxable non-tuition fellowship and stipend payments | Any amounts you exclude from income |

Source : Internal Revenue Service

You can open a Traditional IRA or Roth IRA at any time. You can contribute to your Traditional IRA or Roth IRA at any time during the year or by the due date for filing your income tax return for that year. For most people, the deadline for contributions for a tax year is April 15th of the following year as per the current law.

You can contribute to Traditional or Roth IRA only up to a maximum limit set by the law. The maximum limit may change each year as the law keeps changing. For 2021, the maximum limit for both Traditional IRA and Roth IRA is 6,000 dollars or your taxable compensation, whichever is less. If you are aged 50 and above, you can contribute the lesser of 7,000 dollars or your taxable compensation.

Remember, it is best to contribute up to the maximum allowed to the Traditional IRA or Roth IRA, if possible. That helps to grow your retirement savings quickly through reaping the tax benefits of IRAs.

With the Traditional IRA, you can contribute pre-tax dollars. Your contributions and investment gains grow tax-deferred until your retirement. You will be required to pay taxes on contributions and investment gains when you withdraw funds from your Traditional IRA account during your retirement. Additionally, you may be eligible for tax deduction savings upfront for your contribution amount.

Suppose you are covered by a retirement plan at work. In this scenario, depending on your income, you will get a full deduction, a partial deduction, or no deduction. You will not get a tax deduction if your income exceeds the maximum allowed limit. You are eligible for a full deduction if you (and your spouse if you are married) are not covered by a retirement plan at work.

If you are covered by a retirement plan at work, your income and filing status determines the Traditional IRA tax deduction for 2021 as shown in the following table. You can consult your tax advisor to determine the partial deduction amount if you are eligible for a partial deduction.

| If Your Filing Status Is | And Your Modified Adjusted Gross Income (MAGI) Is | Then You Can Take |
|---|---|---|
| Single or head of household | $66,000 or less | A full deduction up to the amount of your contribution limit |
| | More than $66,000 but less than $76,000 | A partial deduction |
| | $76,000 or more | No deduction |
| Married filing jointly or qualifying widow(er) | $105,000 or less | A full deduction up to the amount of your contribution limit |
| | More than $105,000 but less than $125,000 | A partial deduction |
| | $125,000 or more | No deduction |
| Married filing separately | Less than $10,000 | A partial deduction |
| | $10,000 or more | No deduction |
| If you file separately and did not live with your spouse at any time during the year, your IRA deduction is determined under the "Single" filing status. | | |

Source : Internal Revenue Service

With the Roth IRA, you can contribute your after-tax dollars. The great benefit is you pay no taxes on your contributions and investment gains when you withdraw funds from your Roth IRA account during your retirement years.

In addition to the maximum contribution limit that applies to the Traditional IRA and Roth IRA, the contributions to a Roth IRA can be limited based on your income and filing status. You can contribute to Roth IRA to the full extent only if your income is within a specific limit. The maximum contribution allowed will be reduced above that limit, and you cannot contribute at all if your income exceeds the maximum income limit.

The following table shows the amount you can contribute to Roth IRA for 2021 based on your income and filing status. You can consult your tax advisor to determine the reduced contribution amount if you are eligible for a reduced contribution.

| If Your Filing Status Is | And Your Modified Adjusted Gross Income (MAGI) Is | Then You Can Contribute |
|---|---|---|
| Married filing jointly or qualifying widow(er) | < $198,000 | Up to the limit |
| | ≥ $198,000 but < $208,000 | A reduced amount |
| | ≥ $208,000 | Zero |
| Married filing separately, and you lived with your spouse at any time during the year | < $10,000 | A reduced amount |
| | ≥ $10,000 | Zero |
| Single, head of household, or married filing separately and you did not live with your spouse at any time during the year | < $125,000 | Up to the limit |
| | ≥ $125,000 but < $140,000 | A reduced amount |
| | ≥ $140,000 | Zero |

Source : Internal Revenue Service

You may be wondering what the Modified Adjusted Gross Income (MAGI) is in the above tables. You can calculate Adjusted Gross Income (AGI) by subtracting certain deductions from your total income. You can find your AGI from line 37 on your 1040 tax form. Then you can calculate your MAGI by adding to your AGI, if any, non-taxable Social Security benefits, tax-exempt interest, and unearned foreign income.

For most people, the MAGI will be the same or close to the AGI. There is no line item on the 1040 tax form for your MAGI. However, you can consult your tax advisor to find out your MAGI for a particular tax year to determine your Traditional IRA deduction eligibility or Roth IRA contribution amount.

How do you choose between a Traditional IRA and Roth IRA? As noted earlier, Traditional IRA can be a good option for you if you think you will be in a lower tax bracket during your retirement years. A lower tax bracket means paying taxes at a lower tax rate because you will have lesser taxable income.

In this case, you will not pay taxes now but will pay lower taxes during your retirement. You may want to choose to contribute to the Traditional IRA if you are eligible for upfront tax deduction savings. On the other hand, Roth IRA can be a good option if you will be in a higher tax bracket during your retirement. A higher tax bracket implies paying taxes at a higher tax rate because you will have more taxable income. You may lose some tax credits or deductions and have a higher taxable income during your retirement. In this scenario, you should pay taxes now and be tax-free during your retirement years.

There is no age limit to contribute to a Traditional IRA or Roth IRA. You are required to make minimum amount withdrawals from your 401(k), 403(b), 457(b), SEP IRA or SIMPLE IRA plan or your Traditional IRA once you turn 72 as per the law. You must take minimum amount withdrawals when you reach age 70½ if you turned 70½ before December 31, 2019. You can withdraw more than the minimum amount if you choose. However, the required minimum amount withdrawals do not apply to a Roth IRA.

Supplementing your contributions to the employer-sponsored plan with IRA contributions grows your retirement nest egg at an accelerated pace for you to retire early.

For example, David is making an annual income of 40,000 dollars. He contributes 10% of his salary, or 4,000 dollars, each year to his employer-sponsored 401(k) plan. David wants to get an upfront tax deduction on his contribution and chooses the Traditional IRA option to supplement his retirement savings in the 401(k) plan. Assume he contributes the maximum allowed 6,000 dollars to his Traditional IRA account. With a 7% annual return, David will have a nest egg of 1 million dollars by 55, as shown in the chart to the right.

By supplementing his retirement savings in his 401(k) plan with IRA contributions, David can retire sooner.

## David's Retirement Plan

| Age | 401(k) Contribution | IRA Contribution | Savings Balance |
|-----|---------------------|------------------|-----------------|
| 25 | $4,000 | $6,000 | $10,000 |
| 26 | $4,000 | $6,000 | $20,700 |
| 27 | $4,000 | $6,000 | $32,149 |
| 28 | $4,000 | $6,000 | $44,399 |
| 29 | $4,000 | $6,000 | $57,507 |
| 30 | $4,000 | $6,000 | $71,533 |
| 31 | $4,000 | $6,000 | $86,540 |
| 32 | $4,000 | $6,000 | $102,598 |
| 33 | $4,000 | $6,000 | $119,780 |
| 34 | $4,000 | $6,000 | $138,164 |
| 35 | $4,000 | $6,000 | $157,836 |
| 36 | $4,000 | $6,000 | $178,885 |
| 37 | $4,000 | $6,000 | $201,406 |
| 38 | $4,000 | $6,000 | $225,505 |
| 39 | $4,000 | $6,000 | $251,290 |
| 40 | $4,000 | $6,000 | $278,881 |
| 41 | $4,000 | $6,000 | $308,402 |
| 42 | $4,000 | $6,000 | $339,990 |
| 43 | $4,000 | $6,000 | $373,790 |
| 44 | $4,000 | $6,000 | $409,955 |
| 45 | $4,000 | $6,000 | $448,652 |
| 46 | $4,000 | $6,000 | $490,057 |
| 47 | $4,000 | $6,000 | $534,361 |
| 48 | $4,000 | $6,000 | $581,767 |
| 49 | $4,000 | $6,000 | $632,490 |
| 50 | $4,000 | $6,000 | $686,765 |
| 51 | $4,000 | $6,000 | $744,838 |
| 52 | $4,000 | $6,000 | $806,977 |
| 53 | $4,000 | $6,000 | $873,465 |
| 54 | $4,000 | $6,000 | $944,608 |
| 55 | $4,000 | $6,000 | $1,020,730 |

You may want to keep in mind that there is a possible penalty of 10% for withdrawing the contributions and investment gains from the Traditional IRA account before you reach the age of 59½. For a Roth IRA, the same 10% penalty applies if you withdraw your investment gains before turning 59½. You can withdraw Roth IRA contributions at any time without a penalty. However, do not take out the funds prematurely from the IRAs before turning 59½. So, keep your retirement savings invested for the long term with the compounding effect so you can retire early.

# CHAPTER FIVE

# Contribute Salary Increases and Bonuses in a Retirement Savings Plan

Maybe you are thinking, why not follow the practical plan to start with a small retirement savings contribution and increase the contributions by a set percentage each year? But then, you may have a tight budget that does not allow for additional contributions to your retirement savings plan year after year. In that case, you can consider the following strategies to fund the increase in retirement contributions so that it would not cause a dip in the take-home pay.

You may be able to contribute any salary increases or bonuses you receive from your employer. In addition, you may want to consider contributing to your retirement savings plan any commissions, overtime payments, cash gifts from your friends and family, tax refunds, or stimulus checks.

A lot of credit card companies offer cash rewards as a benefit when you use a credit card. So, you can contribute those credit card cash rewards to the retirement savings plan as well.

Most employers offer salary increases each year to their employees. Suppose if you get a salary increase, you can contribute a portion or all of the salary increases each year to your retirement savings plan. That will avoid a decrease in your take-home pay caused by increasing your retirement contributions. This strategy helps to stick to your budget yet build your retirement nest egg faster and retire sooner.

For example, Mary is 25 years old with an annual income of 40,000 dollars and contributes 10% or 4,000 dollars of her income each year. Her salary goes up by 1% each year. Therefore, she increases her retirement contributions by 1% each year. With a 7% annual return, she will have a retirement nest egg of about one million dollars by 56 years old. This is illustrated in the chart to the right.

In this case, Mary can increase her retirement contributions to her retirement savings plan through her salary increases from her employer. So, she could build her retirement nest egg faster.

## Mary's Retirement Plan

| Age | Salary | Contribution | Savings Balance |
|-----|--------|--------------|-----------------|
| 25 | $40,000 | $4,000 | $4,000 |
| 26 | $40,400 | $4,444 | $8,724 |
| 27 | $40,804 | $4,896 | $14,231 |
| 28 | $41,212 | $5,358 | $20,585 |
| 29 | $41,624 | $5,827 | $27,853 |
| 30 | $42,040 | $6,306 | $36,109 |
| 31 | $42,461 | $6,794 | $45,430 |
| 32 | $42,885 | $7,291 | $55,901 |
| 33 | $43,314 | $7,797 | $67,611 |
| 34 | $43,747 | $8,312 | $80,655 |
| 35 | $44,185 | $8,837 | $95,138 |
| 36 | $44,627 | $9,372 | $111,170 |
| 37 | $45,073 | $9,916 | $128,868 |
| 38 | $45,524 | $10,470 | $148,359 |
| 39 | $45,979 | $11,035 | $169,779 |
| 40 | $46,439 | $11,610 | $193,273 |
| 41 | $46,903 | $12,195 | $218,997 |
| 42 | $47,372 | $12,790 | $247,117 |
| 43 | $47,846 | $13,397 | $277,812 |
| 44 | $48,324 | $14,014 | $311,273 |
| 45 | $48,808 | $14,642 | $347,705 |
| 46 | $49,296 | $15,282 | $387,325 |
| 47 | $49,789 | $15,932 | $430,371 |
| 48 | $50,287 | $16,595 | $477,091 |
| 49 | $50,789 | $17,268 | $527,756 |
| 50 | $51,297 | $17,954 | $582,653 |
| 51 | $51,810 | $18,652 | $642,090 |
| 52 | $52,328 | $19,361 | $706,398 |
| 53 | $52,852 | $20,084 | $775,930 |
| 54 | $53,380 | $20,818 | $851,063 |
| 55 | $53,914 | $21,566 | $932,203 |
| 56 | $54,453 | $22,326 | $1,019,783 |

Suppose you happen to get a yearly bonus from your employer. In that case, you may want to consider contributing a bonus on top of a salary increase to your retirement savings plan. Contributing bonuses and salary increases, if feasible, will allow you to retire even sooner.

For example, Sofia is 25 years old with an annual income of 40,000 dollars and contributes 10% or 4,000 dollars of her income each year. Assume her salary goes up by 1% each year; so, she increases her retirement contributions by 1% each year. Additionally, Sofia contributes her yearly bonus of 2,000 dollars to her retirement savings plan. With a 7% annual return, she will have a nest egg of about one million dollars by the age of 54, as illustrated in the chart to the right.

Sofia amassed a million dollars two years sooner than Mary in the previous example by contributing her yearly bonuses on top of her salary increases to her retirement savings plan.

The more money you invest in a diversified way and the sooner, the better the outcome.

## Sofia's Retirement Plan

| Age | Salary | Contribution | Bonus | Savings Balance |
|-----|--------|--------------|-------|-----------------|
| 25 | $40,000 | $6,000 | $2,000 | $6,000 |
| 26 | $40,400 | $6,444 | $2,000 | $12,864 |
| 27 | $40,804 | $6,896 | $2,000 | $20,661 |
| 28 | $41,212 | $7,358 | $2,000 | $29,465 |
| 29 | $41,624 | $7,827 | $2,000 | $39,355 |
| 30 | $42,040 | $8,306 | $2,000 | $50,416 |
| 31 | $42,461 | $8,794 | $2,000 | $62,738 |
| 32 | $42,885 | $9,291 | $2,000 | $76,421 |
| 33 | $43,314 | $9,797 | $2,000 | $91,567 |
| 34 | $43,747 | $10,312 | $2,000 | $108,288 |
| 35 | $44,185 | $10,837 | $2,000 | $126,705 |
| 36 | $44,627 | $11,372 | $2,000 | $146,946 |
| 37 | $45,073 | $11,916 | $2,000 | $169,149 |
| 38 | $45,524 | $12,470 | $2,000 | $193,460 |
| 39 | $45,979 | $13,035 | $2,000 | $220,037 |
| 40 | $46,439 | $13,610 | $2,000 | $249,049 |
| 41 | $46,903 | $14,195 | $2,000 | $280,677 |
| 42 | $47,372 | $14,790 | $2,000 | $315,115 |
| 43 | $47,846 | $15,397 | $2,000 | $352,570 |
| 44 | $48,324 | $16,014 | $2,000 | $393,264 |
| 45 | $48,808 | $16,642 | $2,000 | $437,435 |
| 46 | $49,296 | $17,282 | $2,000 | $485,337 |
| 47 | $49,789 | $17,932 | $2,000 | $537,243 |
| 48 | $50,287 | $18,595 | $2,000 | $593,444 |
| 49 | $50,789 | $19,268 | $2,000 | $654,254 |
| 50 | $51,297 | $19,954 | $2,000 | $720,006 |
| 51 | $51,810 | $20,652 | $2,000 | $791,058 |
| 52 | $52,328 | $21,361 | $2,000 | $867,793 |
| 53 | $52,852 | $22,084 | $2,000 | $950,623 |
| 54 | $53,380 | $22,818 | $2,000 | $1,039,984 |

# CHAPTER SIX

# Take Advantage of Additional Contributions Allowed if You are Self-Employed

Are you self-employed and looking forward to knowing what your options are for saving for your retirement? You are fortunate. You have many of the same retirement plan options as an employee. Besides, you may have the opportunity of making additional retirement contributions to your retirement plan in an employer capacity.

You can choose from various retirement plan options, including 401(k), Solo 401(k), SIMPLE IRA, and SEP plans.

You can administer a 401(k) plan yourself or take the easier route by outsourcing it to a plan provider. If you do not have any employees, you can open one participant 401(k) plan. The one participant 401(k) plan is known as Solo 401(k), Individual 401(k), or Uni-401(k) plan. You can contribute the pre-tax or after-tax dollars to your retirement plan for the Solo 401(k) and 401(k) options.

More importantly, you can contribute the maximum allowed amount for an employee to your retirement plan. Additionally, you can contribute a maximum allowed percentage of your net earnings as an employer. As per the law for 2021, if you are under age 50, you can contribute a maximum of 19,500 dollars in the employee capacity and can contribute up to a maximum of 25% of your net earnings to the 401(k) plan in the employer capacity. That is a boon for you if you are self-employed and would like to grow your retirement savings quickly with added contributions so that you can retire early.

For example, Christopher is 25 years old and self-employed. He is making yearly earnings of 100,000 dollars; he contributes 19,500 dollars in the employee capacity and an additional 10% of his earnings or 10,000 dollars as an employer. With a 7% annual return, he will have a nest egg of 2 million dollars by age 50, as shown in the chart to the right.

In this scenario, being self-employed helped Christopher to contribute additional savings to his retirement plan.

## Christopher's Retirement Plan

| Age | Employee Contribution | Employer Contribution | Savings Balance |
|---|---|---|---|
| 25 | $19,500 | $10,000 | $29,500 |
| 26 | $19,500 | $10,000 | $61,065 |
| 27 | $19,500 | $10,000 | $94,840 |
| 28 | $19,500 | $10,000 | $130,978 |
| 29 | $19,500 | $10,000 | $169,647 |
| 30 | $19,500 | $10,000 | $211,022 |
| 31 | $19,500 | $10,000 | $255,294 |
| 32 | $19,500 | $10,000 | $302,664 |
| 33 | $19,500 | $10,000 | $353,351 |
| 34 | $19,500 | $10,000 | $407,585 |
| 35 | $19,500 | $10,000 | $465,616 |
| 36 | $19,500 | $10,000 | $527,709 |
| 37 | $19,500 | $10,000 | $594,149 |
| 38 | $19,500 | $10,000 | $665,239 |
| 39 | $19,500 | $10,000 | $741,306 |
| 40 | $19,500 | $10,000 | $822,698 |
| 41 | $19,500 | $10,000 | $909,786 |
| 42 | $19,500 | $10,000 | $1,002,971 |
| 43 | $19,500 | $10,000 | $1,102,679 |
| 44 | $19,500 | $10,000 | $1,209,367 |
| 45 | $19,500 | $10,000 | $1,323,523 |
| 46 | $19,500 | $10,000 | $1,445,669 |
| 47 | $19,500 | $10,000 | $1,576,366 |
| 48 | $19,500 | $10,000 | $1,716,212 |
| 49 | $19,500 | $10,000 | $1,865,847 |
| 50 | $19,500 | $10,000 | $2,025,956 |

As noted earlier, the SEP plan dictates that you need to contribute to your employees' retirement plans at the same rate you have contributed to your retirement plan. However, suppose you have no or few employees. In that scenario, you can contribute up to the maximum allowed percentage of your earnings in your SEP plan to build your retirement nest egg pretty quickly.

For example, Patty is self-employed, making 100,000 dollars net earnings each year. She has no employees and does not have to make employee contributions. Suppose she signed up for a SEP plan and contributes the maximum allowed 25% of her net earnings or 25,000 dollars. With a 7% annual return, Patty will have a retirement nest egg of 2 million dollars by 52 years old. This is shown in the chart to the right.

The idea here is the sooner you save for retirement and the more you contribute to your retirement plan, the more you can grow your retirement savings through reaping the tax benefits of the retirement plan.

## Patty's Retirement Plan

| Age | SEP Contribution | Savings Balance |
|---|---|---|
| 25 | $25,000 | $25,000 |
| 26 | $25,000 | $51,750 |
| 27 | $25,000 | $80,373 |
| 28 | $25,000 | $110,999 |
| 29 | $25,000 | $143,768 |
| 30 | $25,000 | $178,832 |
| 31 | $25,000 | $216,351 |
| 32 | $25,000 | $256,495 |
| 33 | $25,000 | $299,450 |
| 34 | $25,000 | $345,411 |
| 35 | $25,000 | $394,590 |
| 36 | $25,000 | $447,211 |
| 37 | $25,000 | $503,516 |
| 38 | $25,000 | $563,762 |
| 39 | $25,000 | $628,226 |
| 40 | $25,000 | $697,201 |
| 41 | $25,000 | $771,005 |
| 42 | $25,000 | $849,976 |
| 43 | $25,000 | $934,474 |
| 44 | $25,000 | $1,024,887 |
| 45 | $25,000 | $1,121,629 |
| 46 | $25,000 | $1,225,143 |
| 47 | $25,000 | $1,335,904 |
| 48 | $25,000 | $1,454,417 |
| 49 | $25,000 | $1,581,226 |
| 50 | $25,000 | $1,716,912 |
| 51 | $25,000 | $1,862,096 |
| 52 | $25,000 | $2,017,442 |

# CONCLUSION

You have the power to make your Retiring Early dream a reality. Save money early for retirement and make the compounding do the magic for you. You can control your life. You can achieve financial freedom. You can become a millionaire, retire soon, and do the things you enjoy the most. May it be spending leisure time with your family and friends, traveling around the world, reading interesting books, keeping yourself fit, and so on. You can make it all happen. I wish you great success every step of the way on your journey to retiring early.

Made in the USA
Middletown, DE
09 August 2021

45677350R00050